For Faye Pirotta – S.G.
For my own kittens, Chloe and Grace, with love XXX – S.A.

Series concept and design: Liz Black
Book design: Jane Hawkins
Editor: Katie Orchard
Science Consultant: Dr Carol Ballard

Published in Great Britain in 2002 by Hodder Wayland,
an imprint of Hodder Children's Books
Reprinted in 2003

Cataloguing in publication data
Sam Godwin
Rise and Shine: a first look at light. – (Little Bees)
1. Light
I. Title
535

ISBN 07502 3805 4

Printed and bound in Asa, Portugal

Hodder Children's Books
A division of Hodder Headline Limited
338 Euston Road, London NW1 3BH

Rise and Shine

A first look at light

Rise and Shine

A first look at light

Sam Godwin

HODDER
Wayland

an imprint of Hodder Children's Books

It is very early in the morning.

Up with the larks, dear.

Soon the sun rises. Some animals wake up.

Flowers start to open.

9

In the sunlight everything looks

Wow! It's so bright, Mummy.

bright and colourful.

Don't look straight at the sun, dear. It will hurt your eyes.

Where did that worm go?

11

A big cloud floats across the sky.

It hides the sun.

The sun shines brightly again.

That's not a light, dear. It's the sun's reflection.

Who's that handsome frog in there?

The sun shines behind a tree. It makes a big shadow.

It's the end of the day.

The sun begins to set. Flowers close.

19

Soon it gets dark.

People can't see
as well as cats
in the dark.

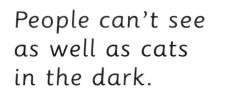

People turn on the lights...

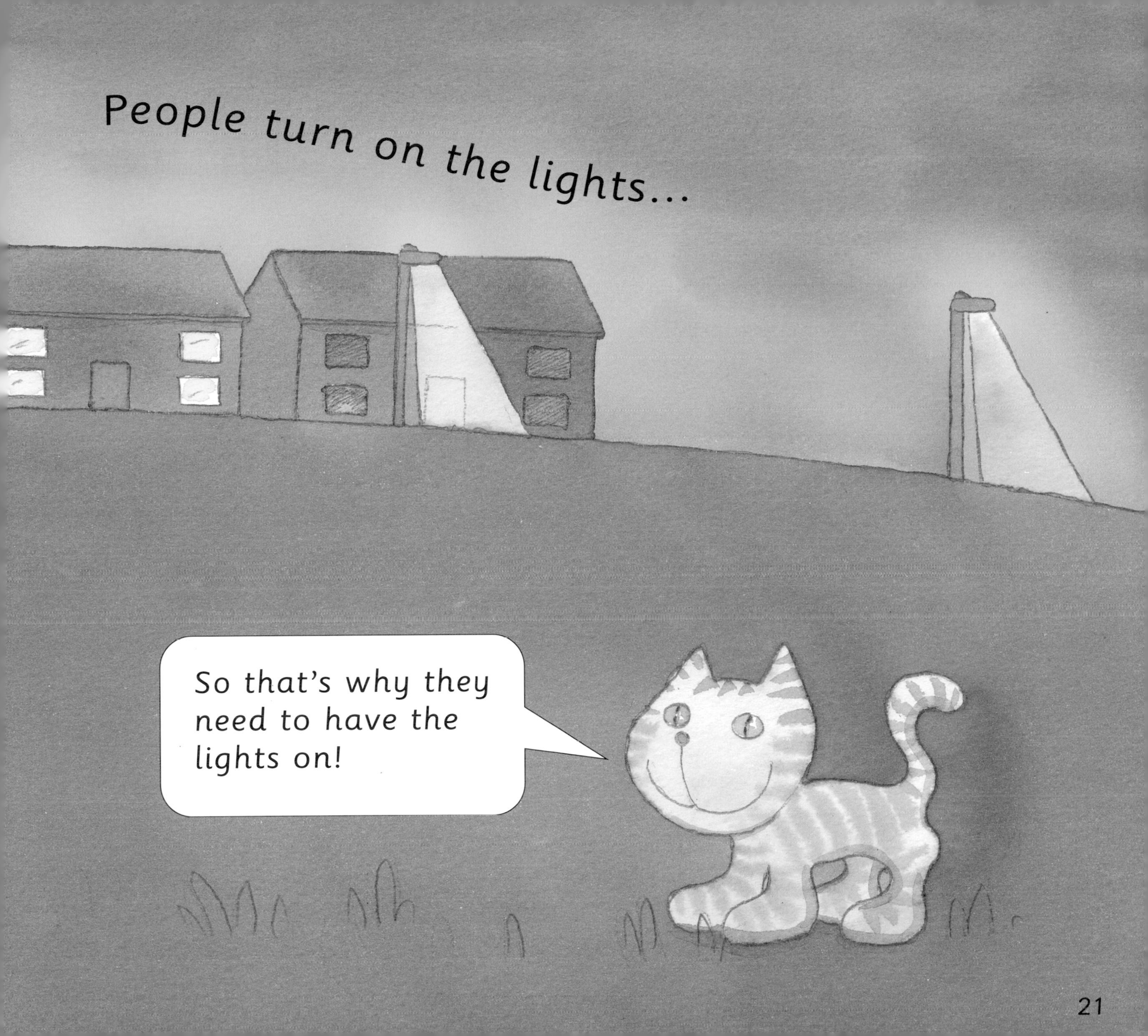

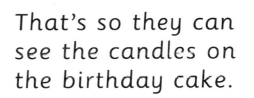

23

When it's dark, people can also use

Oops!

Hurry, dear!
Someone's coming.

torches to light the way.

Who's there?

At night, the moon shines in the sky.

I can see lots of different lights from here.

Some are near and some are far away.

Soon the sun will rise again.

Rise and shine!

It will be another day.

Oh, no!
Not again!

Useful Words

Moon

The moon travels around the Earth. It has no light of its own. It reflects some of the light from the sun.

Reflection

An image that can be seen in a shiny surface, such as a mirror or still water in a pool.

Shadow

When light shines behind an object, it makes a shadow – a dark shape.

Sun

The sun is a star around which the Earth travels. It gives us light and warmth.

Important

The sun's rays are very strong, so:

• Always wear sun cream when you are out in the sun.

• Never look straight at the sun. It will hurt your eyes.

All about light

Light from the sun
makes things look
bright and colourful.

If something covers the
sun, we can't see it any
more. But it's still there.

We can't see the
sun at night.

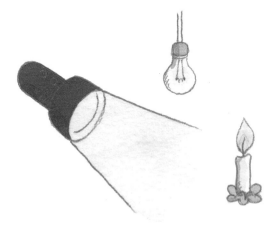

There are lots of different
sources of light.

Shiny surfaces reflect light.